(NO) I AM (NOT) OKAY

(NO) I AM (NOT) OKAY

DRE HILL

<u>Other projects by Dre Hill</u>

i love you means nothing

Melanin: Black

Crossroads

Pushing the Pen: A Poetry Prompt Book

Warning of Content

The following content within this chapbook collection may be triggering, or exacerbate feelings with relation to mental health, mental/emotional crisis, suicide and ideation, depression, and more. Please be advised of these things and keep that in mind. At the end of this book is a small list of available resources to use should you or someone you know require professional assistance.

Table of Contents

Publication Acknowledgements

<u>Hallowzine</u>

this is not pan's labyrinth

in my endless wondering

I wandered too far outside myself

the elements fell upon me first

then the animals

my survival became a defiant act

a stubborn bird to my own mind

as it wished death upon me

to ease my pain

this is not a fantastical world where monsters
and magic roam free or where my problems
fade into the mist and I choose who to be.
there are no reclamations of long-lost lineage
or tainting of the blood of innocents by demons
only the shadow of darkness as it swallows hearts.
this is not a maze of constantly shifting sands
where the breath of the world blows away the
footsteps of my progressive journey forward.
there is no ethereal other world to return where
peace and fantasy rule a land reached only
through the sacrifice of the purest heart.
this is not pan's labyrinth but we still are
the monsters in the stories we tell our kids
as we fail to get them to settle in to bed.
the screams of our youth ring in our ears
as heads beat against the walls of a hell
specially designed by our own bloody hands.
this is not a haunted maze of corn but
the spirits of love lost and undying
whisper to us from within the wall of stalks.
this is not a childhood game of hide and seek
where the biggest fright was being found quickly
because secrets always come to light eventually.
the person I once was is now lost somewhere
between the bloody romances and the
devilish curses spat in the faces of my foes.
this is not pan's labyrinth and yet like a movie
rolls of film unravel to tell the grisly and fantastical
tale of life and all the joys and sorrows it bears.

cross my heart, hope to die

where do you see yourself in 5 years?
alive—*hopefully*
for me the bar is set low
it resides in the hottest pits of hell
the same place that the demons
in my mind come from

my focus narrowed from thriving
to simply surviving
so all I can hope for is to be alive
I realized long ago that—
I don't actually want to die
I just want to experience ease

that's why I don't cross my heart

you've felt like leaving lately
slipping off into the night
carefully cloaked in shadows
much like a master thief
this wouldn't be your first—
contemplation
ideation
attempt

please don't float away
stealing a piece of my heart
in an attempt to soothe yours
there's always another way
stay with me one more day—
breathing
existing
living

black men don't cry

I once forgot how to
cry
my eyes literally dried
up
like tapped reservoirs
my last known release
involved horrifying
mortality
observed at a young
age
my grandmother's
body
ravaged by illness—
was the hollowed shell
that drew my final
tears
then there was nothing
years of endless
dryness
like an unending
famine
my eyes—a desert
land
rough, craggily, and
brittle
they knew no moisture
I in turn, knew no
sadness
there was only the
smile
illuminating for others
while darkening within
an ominous alliance
oppressing my
emotions
my desire to avoid
sadness
joined by societal
conditioning
see—black men don't
cry
we are a diluted
concentrate
there is no room for
tears
amongst macho
mentality
with fragile egos
that—
puff up their chests
proudly
bragging about toxicity
disconnected from
divinity
like an unplugged cord
similarly to so many
others
I remembered how to
cry
when I had my first
breakdown
tears spilled and oozed
snot dribbled as it
pleased
unchecked—unfazed
my reservoir
resurrected
babbling back to life
but, it still came in
spurts
often because I fought
it
like a car in need of
service
tears coughed and
sputtered
they—flirted, with my
eyelashes
as if they were old
acquaintances
I mean, in truth, I
guess they are
friends from a time far
far away
back when I was still
untouched
naïve to the workings
of the world
all because I wanted to
be Spider-Man
long before Miles
Morales was born
my superhero mask
got traded in
for something just as
concealing
yet, somehow even
less revealing
in order to ensure I fit
in with the
silly little mantras of
society like
men are supposed to
be strong
real men don't cry—
toughen up
conceal, don't feel,
don't let it show
long before Disney
had come out
with their catchy
anthem, "Let it Go"

I had already mastered
my emotions
locked away, key
hidden, forgotten
all while they festered
and grew until
they too, could no
longer be contained
instead of refrain I
opted rather to
reframe my thinking—
I cry freely now
because black men do
indeed cry
sometimes singular
streams that
fill thimbles for a
celebratory toast
sometimes it's like
breached dams
that dare to flood
anything tangible
like a baptism—a
watery burial
solemn goodbyes that
are strung
across the skin like
sparkly jewels
worn proudly in the
light of day
in this house—black
men cry
loudly, proudly, often,
and freely
just like breathing on
Sunday mornings

I'm Not Sorry

this is an apology letter
not to you though
there's nothing to apologize for
the gymnastics of your gaslighting
the marathon of your manipulation
the Supplex of my submission
has come to an end.
you got what you deserved
a most glorious fiery end
when you were shot from the sky
only to crash and burn
the flames of retribution coddling you
while agony slices against your lips
like fangs striking the flesh of a rat.
this is an apology letter to myself
for enduring unending delusion
in hopes for grandeur
only to suppress myself in a bottle
like a genie corked in a lamp
lost in the sands of time
as it waits to be freed.

Spiral Szn
(After JoJo)

guess there's ice in the sauvignon
make that vodka—need it strong
island iced tea but make it long
because everything's going wrong
sadly, I have no time to just chill
normally would—but life's going downhill
could treat myself nice but I know I won't
could avoid fighting myself but no I don't
postpone all of my healing
spiral szn is what I'm feeling
loving myself, like that'll ever be enough
ghost of a mantra, when the times get tough
people praise me for what they see—always positivity
they don't know what it's like to live with me—I'm my own enemy
guess there's ice in the sauvignon
make that vodka—need it strong
island iced tea but make it long
because everything's going wrong
sadly, I have no time to just chill
normally would—but life's going downhill
could treat myself nice but I know I won't
could avoid fighting myself but no I don't
postpone all of the healing
spiral szn is what I'm feeling
damn it to hell—overthinking things to death
might just say farewell and give up my last breath
people praise me for what they see—toxic positivity
they don't know what it's like living with me—I'm my worst enemy
guess there's ice in my sauvignon
make that vodka—need it strong
island iced tea but make it long
because everything's going wrong
sadly, I have no time to chill
normally would—life's just going downhill
could treat myself nice but I know I won't
could avoid fighting with myself, but no I don't
postpone all my damn healing

spiral szn is what I'm feeling

spiral season again, yeah

this is my suicide note

you're in disbelief
for that I'm sorry
but, please, recall
the nights I cried
the mountain of lies
a post nut clarity
from the 10-day highs
trying—failing
at keeping my lives separate
my wayward dreams afloat
my light from dimming
so, when you find me
remember this
reflect on my light
the way it shined before
the airborne infection of my laughter
the genius that was praised so highly
please, remember
this note to you
my desire to burn
rising like a newborn phoenix
divvy up my things
carry me in your hearts
and party for me
from dusk until dark

survivor's guilt

it's funny—in an ironic way
how I'm wracked with guilt
about something I could never control
the unchangeable

somehow my helplessness
has locked me into an eternal simulator
reliving every raw moment
like a freshly opened Snapchat

every emotion freshly hits the heart—
coursing through the bloodstream
a waking nightmare that always
starts out as a sleepy daydream

after all—that's how it starts
at first, illusions of normalcy
one minute—combustions of
tragedy and trauma the next

sometimes I pray God takes me

it's said that the toughest battles
are given to God's strongest warriors
I don't know if I'm strong
but I do know—I don't want to be

day after day I wake wondering
why is it that I remain when others are claimed—
why not me? can I not be set free?
is there something else that I cannot see?

my spirit is teetering on the edge,
dangling off the precipice of brokenness,
the softest of breezes just might
push me over it

sometimes I ask that the
good Lord takes me now
only to find myself grateful
for another day of—

sunlight gently kissing my skin

wind whispering secrets to me

life beating inside of my body

you know all your children
by name, but truthfully
probably by heartbeat too
I'll skip the awkward formalities
simply to save us both time
God, it's me, yes again
I know that I always say this
something about it feels right
like I'm real close to you—
like, like you hear my heart
bursting through my chest
as you pat me on the back
massaging comfort into pores
kneading it through tendons
pinched gently into the tissue
hey God, it's me again—

I feel sad and lonely

sometimes I even feel alone
though I'm never lonely
only—because you're here
manifest through blood and bone
both the kind you're born into
as well as the kind you choose
I feel you always around me
in the angels who have no name
who are never actually seen
but their presence is still felt
thank you for that—truly
I would've touched clouds
beyond the ones in my mind
without your touch of heaven
perhaps it's not yet my time
hey God, it's me again—

I'll be back real soon

I killed myself (what now?)

before you jump to any conclusions
let me first dispel any illusions
my body is still very much alive
blood coursing through veins
nervous system still tingling
heart still steadily beating
but, I was buried yesterday
lifeless body—*stiffened bones*
rigor mortis to the old me
broken down and decomposed
old articles to be discarded
it serves me no purpose now
I am not who I was, instead—
I am who I intend on becoming
informed by my past lives
corpses buried near the next
each gravestone is grander
all of them killed by my hand
I guess that makes me a murderer
or does this still count as suicide?
killing your past to birth your future
it's something akin to martyrdom
like being slain for the world's sins
except, I am the world being saved—
at least in this narrative retelling
so I guess I'm only dying for me

the t word

it can feel taboo to say
much less experience it
have you tried the t word?
I'm a big proponent of faith
hope sustained through belief
but you cannot always just pray
expecting the pain to go away
have you tried the t word yet?
sometimes the biggest show
of our faith is seeking help
we have angels on earth
who help heal our hurt
they often go by dr.
go try the t word

nobody talks about the pain that comes from healing. living through an experience is a specifically articulated kind of trauma. to dredge it up, violently opening old wounds, just to pierce the veil with the needle—it's indescribable. my psyche has undergone / lobotomy / all while I remain conscious. acutely aware of each fiber of my being at all times. nauseated by the sensations of the needle threading the skin / the wire pulling flesh together / tightening with each stitch. nobody talks about how much healing hurts—*like damn*. I have never felt so alive / and yet / never wanted to stop feeling more in my life. there were times where I thought I would come undone just to be wound tighter. there's strength in healing. almost like a kind of new growth / like bacteria garnishing a petri dish. with time and treatment, all wounds close. that's the joy and beauty of life, of humanity. I hope you heal—even if it hurts like hell.

50 feet (in my own space)

away from me please
I'm in need of space—
emotional separation
slicing the umbilical cord
that binds me to you
so you can feed off me
perhaps, unintentionally—
though intent doesn't
always matter

I promise I can still hear
when you call from afar
50 feet—outer no space
my vacuum of freedom
an inner sanctuary for
my bleeding heart
sacrificed on the blade
of my empathy—slit open
to satiate your hunger

this is for my own good
revisiting a boundary
I've struggled to uphold
letting you tilt my hand
so I water your flowers
while mine shrivel up
withering from neglect
waiting in agony to die
this I can no longer allow

back up from me please
gon' give me 'bout 50 feet
I need to free my energy
shelter in lone intimacy
you can say whatever
spin whatever narrative
it doesn't matter to me
I'm up in my own space
floating free at last

tired strong friend (who checks on you?)

who checks on you?
my tired strong friend
constant smiler
emotional receptacle
quiet victim of emotions

my tired strong friend
constant smiler
emotional receptacle
quiet victim of emotions
fragile human

constant smiler
emotional receptacle
quiet victim of emotions
fragile human
in need of relief

emotional receptacle
quiet victim of emotions
fragile human
in need of relief
much like a warm, gentle hug

quiet victim of emotions
fragile human
in need of relief
much like a warm, gentle hug
my strong, tired, friend

fragile human
in need of relief
much like a warm, gentle hug
my strong, tired, friend
does anyone check on you?

Amber Mark told me I am worth it

she breathed
existing tangibly
but also in the
ethereal realm of my imagination

her voice reverberates
reaching through my depths
pinging—from blood cell to blood cell
bouncing—along the spidery veins of sinew
sliding—a tingling sensation across the skin

she whispered
exhaling new life
draining the murky pool
that swallowed and forgot me

her arm extends
an offering of salvation
that life can exist
beyond the dark haze

come on, let the love in

cause, baby, you are worth it

(No) I am (not) okay

I won't pretend anymore
choosing to put down my mask
let down my guard—let you in
so when you ask me, I answer in truth
how are you doing?
I am not okay

Today is not a good day
neither was yesterday, actually
but I believe tomorrow will be
it is something that I pray for
quietly, within my mind
like a whispered psalm

sometimes I still feel overwhelmed
drowning slowly in a sea of emotions
wading in the waters of a warring mind
only to remember that I'm not alone
my help is always within reach
I will be just fine

imagine a farewell song
swelling with nostalgia
sweet, staccato notes
striking bitter melodies

take that same song
now stretch it out
infinitely reaching
for the track's end

imagine a farewell song
one that never ends
like an eternal encore
records locked in replay

so take a bow for me
revel in it, my darling
this is your journey
life / broken / by / replay

scars to your beautiful (testimony to living)

sutures hold together my mind
stitches strung along in tight patterns
intricate butterflies spiral in the wind
my scars—a testimony to living
floating fragments of brain matter
wash against the shore of my skull
body parts covered completely
hiding sealed slash marks—
an immortalized record of attempts
but also, of hard fought victories
the scars to your beautiful
skin squirming and scabbing
as the body comes back together
stories etched in the margins
like classic fairytale retellings
of hope waiting in the darkness
whispering gently like the breeze
there's no better you—
than the one that you are
no better life than—
the life that you're living
it's your time to shine—
cuz you're a star
this is your testament
your story of living
there's scars to your beautiful
we're stars and were beautiful

a grateful universe includes you

in all things there is balance
divine harmonic completion
those are my thoughts anyway
how else could all this chaos
not only exist—but coexist
that includes you and I, friend
we are here for a purpose
your existence is justified by
impact on other people
you invoke and maintain balance
something the universe is grateful for
yes we endure hardships unending
but sunshine tastes sweeter after
the sour downpour of rain
I have gratitude in both—
gratefulness in the sunlit breaths
love for the balance of all things, and
solace in the scripture that we will not be alone

If you or a loved one are experiencing a suicide crisis or emotional distress, please consider using the following resources:

The Suicide and Crisis Lifeline

Dial: 988

https://988lifeline.org

Substance Abuse and Mental Health Services Administration

https://www.samhsa.gov/childrens-awareness-day/resources-suicide-prevention

The Trevor Project

https://www.thetrevorproject.org

About the Author

Dre Hill is an artist, storyteller, educator, and apple juice enthusiast from Fort Worth, Tx. He received his BA from Drury University in 2021. He is the author behind i love you means nothing, Melanin: Black, and Crossroads. He is also the creator of the poetry prompt book, Pushing the Pen. When not creating, Dre is often snuggling with his puppy Jet. Find Dre at @drehillart on all platforms. His website is drehillart.com

www.ingramcontent.com/pod-product-compliance
Lightning Source LLC
Chambersburg PA
CBHW060231170726
48004CB00004BA/1504